D1442955

12 QUESTIONS ABOUT
SLAVE NARRATIVES

by Lois Sepahban

www.12StoryLibrary.com

12-Story Library is an imprint of Peterson Publishing Company and Press Room Editions.

Produced for 12-Story Library by Red Line Editorial

Photographs ©: AP Images, cover, 1; Everett Historical/Shutterstock Images, 4, 5, 8, 9, 10, 13, 14, 17, 18, 21, 28; Library of Congress, 6, 7, 22, 24; AS400 DB/Corbis, 11; Henry Louis Stephens/Library of Congress, 12; benoitb/iStockphoto, 15; ilbusca/iStockphoto, 16, 29; Photos.com/Thinkstock, 19; John Vachon/Library of Congress, 23; Amelia P. Lincoln/The Daily Hampshire Gazette/AP Images, 25; Christian Simonpietri/Sygma/Corbis, 26; Jaguar PS/Shutterstock Images, 27

Library of Congress Cataloging-in-Publication Data
Names: Sepahban, Lois, author.
Title: 12 questions about slave narratives / by Lois Sepahban.
Other titles: Twelve questions about slave narratives
Description: Mankato, MN : 12-Story Library, 2017. | Series: Examining primary sources | Includes bibliographical references and index. | Audience: Grades 4-6.
Identifiers: LCCN 2016002344 (print) | LCCN 2016004064 (ebook) | ISBN 9781632352873 (library bound : alk. paper) | ISBN 9781632353375 (pbk. : alk. paper) | ISBN 9781621434542 (hosted ebook)
Subjects: LCSH: Slave narratives--United States--Juvenile literature.
Classification: LCC E444 .S47 2016 (print) | LCC E444 (ebook) | DDC 306.3/620973--dc23
LC record available at http://lccn.loc.gov/2016002344

Printed in the United States of America
Mankato, MN
May, 2016

Access free, up-to-date content on this topic plus a full digital version of this book. Scan the QR code on page 31 or use your school's login at 12StoryLibrary.com.

Table of Contents

What Is a Slave Narrative?

The slave narrative is an autobiographical story of a person's time in captivity. The earliest slave narratives are also called "captive narratives." They were written in the 1500s and 1600s by European travelers who were captured by pirates.

The first North American slave narratives were written before the US Civil War (1861–1865). Some were written by people who were captured in Africa. They were forced into slavery in North America. Some were written by people who were born into slavery.

In North America, slavery was a system that allowed people to buy and sell others and force them

GO TO THE SOURCE

To read examples of slave narratives, go to www.12StoryLibrary.com/primary.

Africans were captured and brought to North America against their will.

to work. The enslaved people came from Africa or the West Indies. Or they were the descendants of people who came from those places. They typically had dark skin. So the institution of slavery in North America was based on a person's skin color and race.

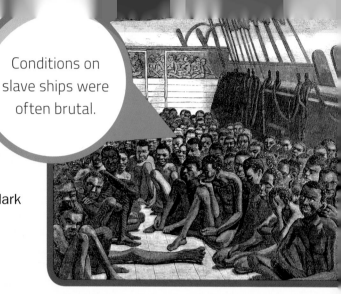

Conditions on slave ships were often brutal.

The purpose of the North American slave narratives was to give a firsthand account of the life of an enslaved person. That makes slave narratives primary sources. These slave narratives are important for two reasons. They document that era of US history from the point of view of enslaved people. And they are the beginnings of African-American literature.

2 million

Approximate number of people captured in Africa and the West Indies and forced into slavery in North America.

- Slave narratives are autobiographical.
- North American slave narratives were written by people captured in Africa and the West Indies and forced into slavery.
- Slave narratives let people today better understand the lives of enslaved people.

WORDS MATTER

The words people choose are important. Using the term "enslaved person" instead of "slave" is a reminder that those forced into slavery were human beings. Using the term "enslaver" instead of "master" does the same. Using the term "slave labor camp" instead of "plantation" is a reminder that enslaved people were forced to work against their will.

Who Wrote Early Slave Narratives?

Many slave narratives include the words "written by himself" or "written by herself." These narratives were different from those that were told to somebody who then wrote the story. Harriet Jacobs was one of the early authors. She was born into slavery in North Carolina sometime around 1813. Unlike most enslaved people, she was taught to read and write when she was a child. In her narrative, she writes, "As a child, I loved my mistress. . . . While I was with her, she taught me to read and spell; and for this . . . I bless her memory."

As a teenager, however, Harriet's life was painful. She was sold to a new family. The man who enslaved her wanted her to have his children. In 1835, she ran away. She spent nearly seven years in hiding. She hid in a tiny attic room at her grandmother's house. It had no windows. During that time, she had little contact with other people. She spent her time reading and thinking and writing.

In the preface of her narrative, she writes that when she was finally free, she couldn't just sit down and write her life story: "Since I have been at the North, it has been necessary for

A cartoon shows President Abraham Lincoln preparing to chop down a tree representing slavery.

A rendering of the Emancipation Proclamation, which Lincoln issued to free enslaved people on January 1, 1863

$100
Amount of money Jacobs was paid for her book.

- Slave narratives are primary sources.
- Jacobs ran away from a life of slavery and then wrote a book about her experiences.
- Her book was published in 1861.

me to work. . . . It has compelled me to write these pages at irregular intervals, whenever I could snatch an hour from household duties." That was how Jacobs wrote her life story. *Incidents in the Life of a Slave Girl* was published in 1861.

Who Was the Audience for Slave Narratives?

North American slave narratives are divided into two groups. Some were written before the US Civil War ended in 1865. Others were written after the war. The audience for each of the groups was different.

The pre-Civil War slave narratives were often written for abolitionists. Abolitionists were people who fought against slavery. They reached out to people who supported slavery or those who had no opinion about it. Abolitionists spoke publicly about the horrors of slavery. They shared the stories of enslaved people in order to convince others that slavery was wrong.

One of these enslaved people was Henry Bibb. *Narrative of the Life and Adventures of Henry Bibb, an American Slave, Written by Himself* was published in 1849. Bibb wanted to work "for the emancipation of

Abolitionists often used emotional appeals to convince others that slavery was wrong.

AM I NOT A MAN AND A BROTHER?

An engraving from Bibb's book shows Bibb and another man being captured after an escape attempt.

my enslaved countrymen." He said that his abolitionist friends asked him to write his story. They wanted the truth about "the sin and evils of slavery" to be heard by other white people. They hoped that white people would join the fight to end slavery when they heard how terrible it was.

Jacobs had a similar goal. But she specifically targeted female readers. In the preface to her narrative, she wrote, "I do earnestly desire to arouse the women of the North to a realizing sense of the condition of two millions of women at the South,

still in bondage, suffering what I suffered, and most of them far worse."

6

Number of letters written by white people that Bibb included in his book to verify that his story was true.

- One important audience for slave narratives was abolitionists.
- Abolitionists fought against slavery.
- Jacobs wanted other women to be moved by her writing.

Why Was Frederick Douglass's Work Important?

One author who chose to share his story was Frederick Douglass. Douglass was born in Maryland in 1818. He was taken from his mother at a young age so that she could work in the fields. She could only visit him from time to time. In his narrative, Douglass wrote:

"She was the only one of all the colored people of Tuckahoe who could read. How she acquired this knowledge, I know not, for Tuckahoe was the last place in the world where she would have been likely to find facilities for learning. . . . I am happy to attribute any love of letters I may have . . . to the genius of my sable, unprotected, uncultivated mother."

Douglass was sold when he was seven or eight years old. At his new home, the wife of the man who enslaved him taught him to read and write. When the woman's husband found out about the lessons, he made her stop. But this made Douglass want to learn even more. From then on, Douglass read whenever he could.

Frederick Douglass

25
Number of years between Douglass's escape from slavery and the signing of the Emancipation Proclamation.

- Douglass shared his story in speeches and in writing.
- He shared his story to help end slavery.
- Speaking out put him in danger of being recaptured.

THINK ABOUT IT

Do you think Douglass's decision to tell his story was an easy one? Why or why not? Using information on these pages, make a list of the things Douglass considered when making his decision.

Douglass escaped from slavery in 1838. Over the next three years, he met white abolitionists. They wanted him to talk about his life in slavery. He became a popular speaker. His words could make his audience cry or laugh. His story made a powerful case against slavery.

Because Douglass spoke and wrote like an educated man, many white people didn't believe his story was true. In order to prove that he was telling the truth, Douglass had to take a big risk. He had to identify the man who had enslaved him. This was dangerous. The man who had enslaved Douglass wanted him back. But Douglass believed that telling his story was worth the risk. He remained free, and his book *Narrative of the Life of Frederick Douglass* was published in 1845.

Title page and portrait of the author from Douglass's first book

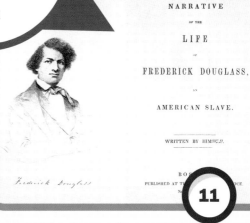

NARRATIVE

OF THE

LIFE

OF

FREDERICK DOUGLASS,

AN

AMERICAN SLAVE.

WRITTEN BY HIMSELF.

BOS...
PUBLISHED AT T...

Frederick Douglass

5

Why Were Stories about Slave Auctions Important?

Slave auctions are an important part of slave narratives. Slave auctions were markets where people were bought and sold. At these auctions, people were treated like animals. They were often forced to stand naked in front of a crowd. Enslavers who wanted to buy them would inspect their mouths or other parts of their bodies. Then, they would bid on them.

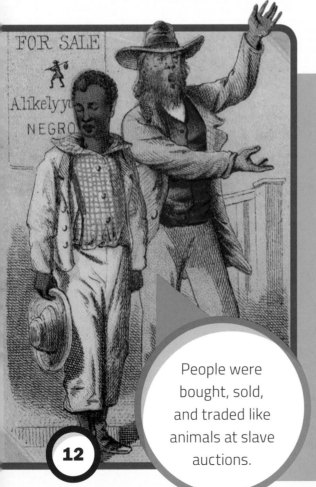

People were bought, sold, and traded like animals at slave auctions.

THE LIFE OF OLAUDAH EQUIANO

Olaudah Equiano was a freed slave living in England. His autobiography, *The Interesting Narrative of the Life of Olaudah Equiano*, was published in 1789. It is one of the few narratives that describes the Middle Passage. This was the dangerous crossing from Africa to North America. Captured Africans were chained together, beaten, and starved during the trip. Many died. Those who survived were sold into slavery.

Not all enslaved people were sold at auctions. But it was something they all feared. Being sold at a slave auction meant being separated from your family and friends. It was a humiliating experience. It was designed to make enslaved people feel less than human. Telling stories about the slave auctions helped to reinforce the horrors faced by enslaved people.

In the 1930s, former enslaved people such as Delia Garlic and W. L. Bost told their stories. Garlic said that babies were

This image of a slave auction came from an 1834 book written by an abolitionist.

100

Age of Garlic when she told her story about slave auctions.

- Slave auctions were markets where people were bought and sold.
- Slave auctions were humiliating.
- Slave auctions broke families apart.

taken from their mothers and sold. Children were separated from brothers and sisters and "never saw each other" again. Bost recalled auctions that were held in the winter. He remembered how the enslaved people were chained together. They didn't have warm clothes or shoes. When they got too cold, they were forced to run to keep warm.

How Did Slavery Affect Families?

Slavery did not respect family bonds. Enslaved people might marry and have children. But there were no guarantees the family would stay together. At any moment, parents or children could be sold, never to see each other again.

This constant threat to their families did not stop enslaved people from forming loving and deep bonds. For decades after the Civil War ended, former enslaved people advertised in newspapers. They were looking for their family members who had been sold away.

Slave narratives are filled with stories of family. In the 1930s, Laura Clark described being sold when she was six or seven years old. When Clark was loaded onto the wagon, her mother collapsed on the ground crying. That was the last time Clark ever saw her.

Douglass said that he knew "nothing" about his father. In his

Many enslaved people were separated from their loved ones. This five-generation family was an exception.

A mother clings to her daughter in this depiction of a slave auction.

story, he wrote that "slavery had no recognition of fathers, as none of families." Few enslaved children grew up with their fathers. Marshall Butler remembered that his father didn't get to live with him and his mother until after the war. And Sarah Frances Shaw Graves said that when she was about six months old, she and her mother were taken from Kentucky to Missouri. Her father stayed in Kentucky, "as he belonged to another man." They never saw him again.

4 million
Approximate number of people who were enslaved in the South in 1861.

- Families were often broken apart because of slavery.
- Children were taken away from their mothers.
- Fathers often were not part of their children's lives.

ENSLAVED CHILDREN

In *Up from Slavery*, educator Booker T. Washington described the life of a typical enslaved child. Washington's mother had to work all day, so he only saw her early in the morning or late at night. He never played games or sports. He was forced to work "almost every day" of his life. He had to clean, "carry water to the men," or take corn to the mill that was three miles away. Washington was nine years old when slavery was abolished in the United States.

How Was Labor Described in Slave Narratives?

Many enslaved people performed back-breaking work in the hot sun all day long.

Enslaved people engaged in unpaid forced labor. The work was physically hard and the workday was long. Most enslaved people in the South worked on farms. They raised crops such as cotton, rice, and tobacco. In the 1930s, Sarah Gudger described her life as an enslaved person. She said that she never knew anything but work. She worked from morning until late at night. Her work was

$100
Amount of money Sojourner Truth was sold for in 1806. In 2015, that would be approximately $1,500.

- Enslaved people were not paid for their work.
- Some enslaved people worked inside the house.
- Most enslaved people worked outside on farms.

CHILDREN AS ENSLAVERS

It was common to give a young white child another child to enslave. Martin Jackson remembered that when he was about five years old, he was given to the two-year-old son of the man who enslaved his family. This meant that he became the property of a two-year-old child. His job was to keep the two-year-old company and help take care of him.

mostly outside. She had to do whatever she was told to do. She had to work in the fields, chop wood, and hoe the garden. She worked until she felt like her back would break. She was forced to work even in bad weather. In the winter, she had to go up into the mountains to cut trees. Then, she would drag them down to be used in the house.

Some enslaved people worked inside the house. They worked as servants—maids, butlers, and cooks. In Sojourner Truth's story, *A Bondswoman of Olden Time*, she remembered when she was sold at nine years old. She said, "Now the war begun." She meant that this was when all of her suffering really began. She described her work in the house and how she was beaten when she didn't understand what she was supposed to do.

Jenny Proctor was also forced to work inside the house. She remembered that her mother, who was the cook, had to get up at 3:00 a.m. to start preparing breakfast. She said that as soon as she was big enough, she had to help clean the house.

Sojourner Truth

Why Were Stories of Escape Told?

Escape was a constant in the lives of enslaved people. They whispered about others who had gotten away. They thought about escaping themselves. Many enslaved people ran away. Sometimes, they were successful. Sometimes, they were not.

Enslaved people had two main obstacles to running away. The first was that they might be caught. If they were caught, their punishment was severe. They might be attacked by dogs. And they were certain to be whipped badly, sometimes to death. The second obstacle was fear for their family. Anyone left behind would likely be punished by the people who enslaved them.

In spite of these fears, enslaved people still ran away. Harriet Tubman described how she made her decision: "There was one of two things I had a right to, liberty or death; if I could not have one, I would have the other." Once she

Armed fugitive slaves defend themselves against slave catchers in Maryland in 1855.

Many enslaved people escaped to the North via the Underground Railroad.

made it to safety in 1849, she sent a message to her family that she was free.

Telling the story of her escape to safety would have an important impact on her life. She had friends and family members who were still enslaved. They heard Tubman's story and wanted to escape, too. In 1850, Tubman returned to the place where she had been enslaved. It was her first trip on the Underground Railroad. The Underground Railroad was a network of safe houses for runaways to shelter in and get help on their journey to freedom. She went to help her family members escape to freedom.

13
Number of trips Tubman made to the South to help enslaved people run away.

- Running away from slavery was dangerous.
- If runaways were caught, their punishment was harsh.
- Runaways worried that their family members might be punished.

THINK ABOUT IT

Do you think running away from slavery was a good idea? Write a paragraph explaining your argument. Use evidence from these pages to support your viewpoint.

9

How Did Emancipation Affect Slave Narratives?

Emancipation was the moment an enslaved person was set free. This could have happened at any time during the period of slavery in the United States. Sometimes, enslaved people were freed when the men or women who owned them died. Sometimes, they were freed when purchased and released by a buyer.

President Abraham Lincoln signed the Emancipation Proclamation on January 1, 1863. That act made slavery illegal in many areas. But people weren't really free until after the war. The 13th Amendment to the US Constitution finally ended slavery in the United States when it was ratified in December 1865.

The stories told after 1865 show how life after emancipation was still difficult for people who had been enslaved. One problem was the racism directed toward black people across the United States. This racism made it difficult for former enslaved people to get jobs that paid fairly. They struggled to find affordable housing.

Julia Williams spoke about this hard time. She said that many former enslaved people were forced "to stay on [the] plantation," working for very little money. Some were afraid to leave because they didn't know

11

Number of Confederate slave-owning states during the Civil War.

- Emancipation was when enslaved people were given their freedom.
- All people were free after the 13th Amendment was ratified.
- Former enslaved people had to start new lives with nothing.

Many depictions of slavery from a southern viewpoint made it appear that white owners took good care of the people they enslaved.

where else to go. Some were unable to get work. Many decided their best option was to farm as sharecroppers for former slave owners.

Postwar narratives also were important because many southern writers were publishing books that romanticized slavery in the South.

They made it seem like slavery wasn't as bad as people thought. They depicted the days of slavery as the "good old days." Post-war slave narratives showed the truth of the days of slavery. The details gave clear descriptions of the cruelties of slavery.

Why Were Slave Narratives Collected in the 1930s?

Between 1936 and 1938, the US government hired people to interview former enslaved people. Over the two-year period, interviewers visited 17 states. They interviewed more than 2,000 former enslaved people.

This was an enormous job, and it was important. Time was running out.

Most of the people interviewed were at least 80 years old. That meant that if the stories of former enslaved people were going to be recorded, it had to be done soon.

The stories collected by the Federal Writers' Project were published in a book titled *Slave Narratives: A Folk History of Slavery in the United States from Interviews with Former Slaves*. These narratives provided first-person accounts of people who had been enslaved. They were different from the slave narratives published in the 1700s and 1800s. The purpose of those early narratives was to help end slavery. The purpose of these stories was to record the lives of enslaved people.

When Arthur Greene was interviewed, he asked, "What makes

The Federal Writers' Project captured the stories and images of hundreds of former enslaved people in the late 1930s.

you folks wait so long before you [get] this stuff about way back yonder?" He understood that time was running out to record the stories. And when Gudger was interviewed, she said, "I ain't [telling] no lies." It was important to the former enslaved people that their stories be recorded and that the world know that their stories were the truth.

A young black boy drinks from a "colored" fountain in North Carolina in 1938.

COLORED

71

Number of years that had passed since the end of the Civil War and when the interviewers started their work.

- Starting in 1936, the US government paid workers to interview former enslaved people.
- The interviews were collected in *Slave Narratives: A Folk History of Slavery in the United States from Interviews with Former Slaves.*
- These interviews are primary source documents that describe what life was like for enslaved people.

JIM CROW

Jim Crow was the name given to the unfair and racist system in the South that started after the Civil War ended. Under Jim Crow laws, it was almost impossible for black people to vote. Public life was segregated. That meant that black people could not do many things white people could. They couldn't sit in the same seats or drink from the same water fountains. Black people had to go to separate schools and hospitals. It was another way to deny black people their rights long after slavery had ended. The Civil Rights Act of 1964 helped put an end to Jim Crow.

What Can We Learn from Slave Narrative Viewpoints?

As primary sources, slave narratives give details and descriptions of times past. These first-person accounts tell us about times we can't revisit and places we can't travel to. The language choices used in the narratives tell us something about the education of the author. The way that certain phrases are repeated, like "the true account," tells us about how important it was to the author that we believe his or her story.

Narratives that were "written by himself" or "written by herself" are different from narratives that were written by someone else. The narratives of Olaudah Equiano and Harriet Jacobs are told from a first-person point

Title page from Equiano's narrative

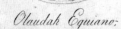

THE

INTERESTING NARRATIVE

OF

THE LIFE

OF

OLAUDAH EQUIANO,

OR

GUSTAVUS VASSA,

THE AFRICAN.

WRITTEN BY HIMSELF.

Behold, God is my salvation; I will trust, and not be afraid, for the Lord Jehovah is my strength and my song; he also is become my salvation.
And in that day shall ye say, Praise the Lord, call upon his name, declare his doings among the people. Isa. xii. 2. 4.

EIGHTH EDITION ENLARGED.

NORWICH:

PRINTED FOR, AND SOLD BY THE AUTHOR.

1794.

PRICE FOUR SHILLINGS.

Formerly sold for 7s.

Olaudah Equiano:

23
Number of audio-recorded interviews of former enslaved people held in the Library of Congress.

- The words authors used in their narratives tell us about their purpose.
- Primary sources such as slave narratives teach us about the past.
- It is important to consider how an interviewer might affect an interview.

of view. Because of this, Equiano's and Jacobs's narratives read like diaries. Sojourner Truth's story was written by someone else. She told her story to Frances W. Titus, a white woman who lived in New York. Even though the story is told by Truth herself, it is told from a third-person point of view. It might not feel as intimate to some readers as a first-person narrative.

It is also important to pay attention to the interviewers who recorded stories in the 1930s. Most of the interviewers were white. Historians wonder how the former enslaved

people's stories might have been different if the interviewers had been black, too. They wonder if the former enslaved people may have "self-censored" during the interviews. This means that they didn't tell the interviewers everything, because they didn't know how the interviewers would interpret their words.

A statue of Truth was unveiled in Northampton, Massachusetts, in 2002.

What Is the Impact of Slave Narratives Today?

Slave narratives changed the way people thought about slavery in North America. Their impact can still be felt today. Leaders of the civil rights movement in the mid-twentieth century followed the slave narrative model to remind people that black Americans were still not truly free. *The Autobiography of Malcolm X* was written in a form similar to the early slave narratives. The speeches of Dr. Martin Luther King Jr. were reminiscent of Douglass's powerful style of speaking. These leaders used their stories to build support from black and white Americans for the civil rights cause.

The earliest slave narratives influenced future generations of black American writers and filmmakers. Solomon Northup's narrative, published in 1853, became the basis for the movie *12 Years a Slave* in 2013. Toni Morrison's 1987 novel *Beloved* was inspired by the true story of a

Author Alex Haley (center) poses with two actresses on the set of the hit TV miniseries *Roots*.

woman who escaped slavery. Alice Walker won the Pulitzer Prize for Fiction in 1983 for her novel *The Color Purple*. Both of those books were turned into popular movies.

And Alex Haley created a national sensation with his novel *Roots*. This work of historical fiction told the story of seven generations of a black family, spanning from Africa to North America. The book was turned into an award-winning miniseries in 1977. More than 100 million Americans watched it. It was the first time many white Americans had confronted the horrors of slavery. These stories ask their audiences to examine the historical oppression of black people and compare it to conditions in modern times.

Actress Lupita Nyong'o won an Academy Award for her portrayal of an enslaved woman in the 2013 movie *12 Years a Slave*.

1870

Year that black men were given the right to vote by the 15th Amendment.

- Slave narratives helped change the way people viewed slavery.
- They inspired the work of civil rights leaders.
- Modern film and literature reflect these narratives.

THINK ABOUT IT

What do you think are two important effects the slave narratives had? Find evidence in this chapter to support your ideas.

Fact Sheet

- Some enslaved people chose to tell their stories in unusual ways. Dave Drake, also known as Dave the Potter, lived in Edgefield, South Carolina, from around 1801 until the 1870s. He was known for writing short messages into the wet clay of the pottery he made. These messages include, "I made this jar." His work was important because it was illegal for enslaved people to be taught to read and write at the time. Drake wrote his messages anyway. Today, his work is quite valuable.

- Historically, slave narratives had three common forms. One form was the story of religious redemption. In this form, the person who had been enslaved used religious themes and myths to tell their story. A second form was a story that inspired the abolitionist struggle. In this form, the person who had been enslaved used the narrative to encourage abolitionists to continue fighting for an end to slavery. A third form was the story of progress. In this form, the person who had been enslaved used the narrative to describe how he or she became stronger or educated or independent after finding freedom.

- The Library of Congress's 23 audio recordings of interviews with people who were born into slavery are the only such recordings known to exist. The interviews total almost seven hours. The earliest was recorded in 1932, and the last was recorded in 1975.

- The Library of Congress has approximately 2,300 written interviews and 500 photographs of people who had been enslaved. These were collected between 1936 and 1938 through the Works Progress Administration's Federal Writers' Project.

Glossary

abolitionist
A person in favor of ending slavery.

account
A statement of facts.

audience
A group that listens to or reads what has been said.

autobiography
A biography written by the person it is about.

bond
A binding connection between people.

captivity
A situation where one is prevented from being free.

generation
The people in a family born at about the same time.

institution
An established custom or practice.

narrative
Something that is told or written.

preface
An introduction to a book, typically stating its subject, scope, or aims.

publicly
In front of other people.

ratify
To approve by vote.

sharecroppers
Farmers who give a portion of their crops to the owner of the land they rent.

threat
Something that might cause harm.

For More Information

Books

Altman, Linda Jacobs. *Slavery and Abolition in American History*. Berkeley Heights, NJ: Enslow Publishers, 2015.

Blashfield, Jean F. *Slavery in America*. New York: Children's Press, 2012.

Hall, Brianna. *Freedom from Slavery: Causes and Effects of the Emancipation Proclamation*. North Mankato, MN: Capstone Press, 2014.

Index

About the Author

Lois Sepahban has written several books for children. Her favorite books to write are about science and history, biographies, and fiction. She lives in Kentucky with her husband and two children.